The Uniqueness of Our Calling

The Uniqueness of Our Calling

William B. Hallman
(1903-1973)

BIBLE STUDENT'S PRESS™
Windber, Pennsylvania

The Uniqueness of Our Calling
by William B. Hallman (1903-1973)

Executive Editor: André Sneidar

Cover design by Nathan Hyde Pilkington

ISBN: 978-1-62904-600-6

Published by

Bible Student's Press™
An imprint of *Pilkington & Sons*
P.O. Box 265
Windber, PA 15963

For other titles by the author, visit
www.ClydePilkington.com

For information on *Bible Student's Press*™ releases, visit:
www.BibleStudentsPress.com

For information on other Bible study resources, visit:
www.StudyShelf.com

Printed in the United States of America.

CONTENTS

1. Dispensation – Mystery – Church (Oikonomia – Musterion – Ekklesia)............9

2. Paul's Two Ministries (Before and After Acts 28) 17

3. Paul's Unique Latter Ministry (Unique Dispensation – Unique Dynamic – Unique Destiny) 25

Chapter 1

Dispensation - Mystery - Church (Oikonomia - Musterion - Ekklesia)

Two passages of Scripture form the foundation for this message. First a verse from Paul's letter to the Ephesians, in a free translation of my own:

> ... *To enlighten all as to what is the Dispensation of the Secret which has been hidden from the ages in God Who created all things by Jesus Christ* (Ephesians 3:9).

The second verse is from the same apostle's letter to the Colossians:

> ... *For His Body's sake, which is the church; of which I became a servant according to the Dispensation of God which is given to me for you to complete the Word of God: even the Secret which has been hid from the ages and from the generations but now*

is made manifest to His saints. To whom God did will to make known what the riches of the glory of this Secret are among the Nations which is Christ among you, the hope of glory (Colossians 1:24-27).

There are three Greek words in these verses which form the basis for any study in the Bible. The first we shall discuss is the word we usually speak of in English as *"dispensation"* or *"administration."* These are good translations of the original word.

The second word that we need to carefully understand is the word *"mystery"* or *"secret."* There is more than one mystery mentioned and revealed in the Bible. Which one is it that belongs to us?

The third word is *"church"* or *"assembly."* There are many assemblies (*ecclesia*) in the Bible, and we need to know to which assembly we really belong. Let us examine each of these three key words in turn.

DISPENSATION

There are three forms of this particular word as we translate it into English, and these words occur a total of twenty times in our New Testament. In the *Authorized Version* they are translated by such words as: steward, stewardship, dispensation, and once each, Godly edifying, chamberlain, and governors.

So we have a conglomeration of English words with reference to the translation of *"dispensation."*

Oikonomia

Oikonomia is made up of two Greek words: *oikos,* which is the Greek word for "house," and *nemo,* which means to "dispense." Put the two together and you have a word which means literally "house dispensing," or something which is distributed or dispensed in and from a house.

Nine times in the New Testament this basic Greek word for dispensation is used, which means to parcel out, distribute, manage. It occurs three times in Luke's gospel (16:2-4); once in I Corinthians 9:17; three times in Ephesians 1:10; 3:2, 9; once in Colossians 1:25; once in I Timothy 1:4.

Oikonomos

Oikonomos is a combination of *oikos,* meaning "house," and *nomos,* meaning "rule" – thus "house rule." It can also refer to the "house ruler," someone particularly chosen to dispense.

This word occurs ten times in the New Testament. It is used by Luke in his gospel (12:42; 6:1, 3, 8). It occurs in Romans 16:23; in I Corinthians 4:1-2 and once each in Galatians 4:2; Titus 1:7; I Peter 4:10.

Oikonomeo

Oikonomeo occurs only once in the Bible, in Luke 16:2. It is in the form of an infinitive verb and means literally "to be a steward."

Different Dispensations

There is a sense in which the Bible is given to us for knowledge and understanding, but not in the sense of *dispensation*. A dispensation limits truth. It is a house rule.

Some people read the Bible and then sing the chorus, "Every promise in the Book is mine." This is absolutely unscriptural.

God told Noah to do a certain thing. Has He told me to do the same thing? God told Abraham to do certain things. Has He told me to do the same things?

Later on we will discuss the Dispensation in which we live and will develop it further. It is basic, however, to see that the word dispensation does not mean a time period. There may be more than one dispensation in a certain age. For example, we have the word *chronos*, which has reference to "time." We have the word *kairos*, which should be translated "*season.*" We have the word *aion*, which should be translated "*age.*" These are all different words so that a dispensation does not necessarily have the time element within it. It is something that is dispensed within time.

We have some biblical examples of those who dispense a dispensation – *i.e.,* dispensationalists. For example, there was Eliezer, the steward in Abraham's house (Genesis 15:2). We are told in Genesis 24:2 that he was a ruler in the house. He was a dispenser and he was a ruler: a true *oikonomos* over a true *oikonomia.*

We could also mention Joseph, who was an overseer. He was chosen by Pharaoh to distribute grain in the time of famine. We are also told that he was given the second highest rank of rulership over the country of Egypt.

It is important to understand the meaning of the word dispensation and to see what we are to dispense in this dispensation. There are many people who are afraid of the word. Some are anti-dispensationalist and some would dub us extreme dispensationalists. However, anyone who has ever read the Scriptures must recognize that there is such a word and that it has a scriptural meaning. Therefore no one who teaches the Word can truly be anti-dispensational.

MYSTERY

The second word, *"mystery"* or *"secret"* is a translation of the Greek word *musterion*. In its modern usage we think of something that is a mystery as something which cannot be understood. In the biblical sense, however, it is something that cannot be understood until or unless it is *revealed*.

The word *"mystery"* is used 27 times in the New Testament: three times in the gospels, 20 times in Paul's epistles, and four times in Revelation.

There are many mysteries in the Bible. For example the mysteries of the Kingdom (Matthew 13); the mystery of the duration of Israel's blindness (Romans 11); the mystery of iniquity (II Thessalonians 2:7); the mystery of Godliness; the mystery of the seven stars; the mystery of God; the mystery of Babylon the Great; the mystery of the woman (all these in Revelation); and finally, the mystery revealed in Ephesians and Colossians.

The mystery of Ephesians and Colossians must be distinguished from all of the other mysteries. Paul revealed the Secret for the day in which we live. The other mysteries do not belong to us today.

CHURCH

The Greek word for "church" or "assembly" is *ekklesia*, which comes from two words: *ek* (out of) and *kaleo* (to call forth). There are various "churches" in the Scriptures. For example, we have *"the church in the wilderness"* (Acts 7:38) with reference to Israel. There is the *"church of God"* mentioned in Acts and nearly all of Paul's early epistles (which are usually called Acts-period epistles).

We also see many local churches in the New Testament: the church which is at Jerusalem, the church of the Thessalonians, churches in certain provinces, churches which met in private homes. There were churches of Galatia, Asia, Macedonia, Judea, Ephesus, Smyrna, Pergamos, Thyatira, Sardis, Philadelphia and Laodicea; and of course there is the church, the Body of Christ.

We can see that, with such a mass of Scripture in reference to the word *ekklesia*, we have to ask, "Which one refers to the church in which we have a part today?"

It is important that we see the distinctiveness of the three words (dispensation, mystery and church) as basic to an understanding of any position in the Bible and particularly to ours.

Chapter 2

Paul's Two Ministries (Before and After Acts 28)

Another foundation point is the fact of Paul's two-fold ministry. We are not going to see the uniqueness of our position until we see Paul's two ministries. This is where I believe that most dispensationalists fail.[1] Here are some Bible references to show what the Scriptures say about Paul's two-fold ministry.

First of all, in Acts 20:27 Paul says:

> *I have not shunned to declare unto you all the counsel of God.*

Does this include the revelations of his prison ministry?

---

1. Two books which are absolutely essential to this study are Charles H. Welch's *Apostle of the Reconciliation* and *From Pentecost to Prison*, both dealing with the book of Acts. [**Editor**: see order form.]

Let us go on a little further to Acts 26:16, where he is rehearsing his conversion and relating what the Lord spoke to him:

*But rise and stand upon thy feet, for I have appeared unto thee for this purpose to make thee a minister and a witness, **both** of these things which thou hast seen, and of those things in the which I will appear unto thee.*

When we hear the word *"both"* we know that there are two separate things spoken of. Paul had seen some things that he was to reveal, and he was going to receive a further revelation to which he would witness.

Reading further in Acts 26 we find that Paul declares,

*… having therefore obtained help of God, I continue unto this day, witnessing both to small and great, **saying none other things than those which the Prophets and Moses did say should come;** that Christ should suffer and that He should be the first that should rise from the dead and should show light*

unto the people and to the Gentiles.

Up to that time, Paul was witnessing to things written in the Old Testament Scriptures.

One final verse in Acts 28:20 completes this picture of Paul's first ministry:

*For this cause therefore have I called for you, to see you and to speak with you because that **for the Hope of Israel I am bound with this chain.***

In light of those passages let us now refer to a couple of others from Ephesians and Colossians:

For this cause, I Paul, the prisoner of Jesus Christ for you Gentiles ... that the Gentiles should be fellow heirs and of the same body and partakers of His promise in Christ by the Gospel whereof I was made a minister (Ephesians 3:1, 6-7).

Whereof I am made a minister according to the dispensation of God which is given to me for you to fulfill the Word of

God, even the mystery which hath been hid from ages and from generations but now is made manifest to His saints (Colossians 1:25-26).

You will seek in vain for a statement like that in the Law or the Prophets. Neither Moses nor the Prophets knew anything about these new truths.

If Paul were still preaching the Prophets and Moses, how could he say that it was *"hid from the ages and from generation"* of the past?

If we are careful in our reading, we must come to the conclusion that Paul has an *early* ministry during the book of Acts in which he ministers the truth as it was found in the Old Testament. Yet when he comes to his *latter* ministry he is revealing something that is different.

Some say that all he did was to add something to the former. This is not quite true, according to the revelation. It isn't an *evolution* from Judaism that we are in today. It isn't something that has been *added* to the revelation that God gave to Israel.

BEFORE AND AFTER ACTS 28

In a pamphlet entitled *Before and After Acts 28,* J. Eustice Mills[2] lists over a dozen differences between Paul's early and later ministries. Here are some to consider:

1. – During the Acts period, Israel is urged to *"turn again"* (repent) in order that God might *"send the Christ even Jesus"* (Acts 3:12-21).

Ye men of Israel, turn again that He may send the Christ Who hath been appointed for you, even Jesus.

That is what Peter said on the day of Pentecost. After the book of Acts, Israel's hope of the Lord's return was deferred, for Paul declared in the words of Isaiah that their heart was hardened. They became dull of hearing, and they became blind.

---

2. **[*Editor:*]** We have not as of yet been able to locate this pamphlet. However, our readers may benefit from an article by the same title by Oscar Baker found in *Bible Student's Notebook #595.*

   We have run other articles by J. Eustice Mills in past *Bible Student's Notebook* issues:

   #701: "The New Covenant" Part 1,

   #725: "The New Covenant" Part 2,

   #726: "The New Covenant" Part 3.

For the heart of this people has waxed gross, their ears are dull of hearing, their eyes have been closed, lest they should see with their eyes and hear with their ears and understand with their heart and should be converted (Acts 28:27).

The judgment passed upon Israel said only one thing – that their opportunity had ceased, although only temporarily. God has a future purpose for Israel, but for the time being, since Paul pronounced the judgment, the fulfillment of Isaiah 6 has been for Israel what Hosea calls *Lo-Ammi* – "*not My people.*"

2. – During the Acts period the word of salvation was *"sent"* to Israel with a warning concerning what might come upon them if they failed to give heed.

Children of the stock of Abraham, whoever among you feareth God, to you is the word of this salvation sent. ... Beware therefore, lest that come upon you which is spoken of in the prophets (Acts 13:26, 40).

That doesn't sound like truth for today, does it?

After Acts, the salvation of God was sent to the Gentiles in consequence of Israel's failure. In Acts 28:28 Paul declares:

> *Be it known, therefore unto you that the salvation of God is sent unto the Gentiles and they will hear it.*

This is entirely a different sending.

3. – During Acts, believing Gentiles such as Cornelius were permitted to partake of *"the Word which God had sent unto the children of Israel"* (Acts 10:36).

After Acts the Gentiles received the Word which God by revelation sent unto them: the Dispensation of the Secret. We read,

> *You Gentiles, since you have heard of the Dispensation of the Grace of God which is given to me to youward, that by revelation He made known to me the Secret* (Ephesians 3:2-3).

4. During the period of the Acts, Paul was bound for *"the hope of Israel."*

Because that for the hope of Israel I am bound with this chain (Acts 28:20).

After Acts, he became a prisoner of Jesus Christ for the Gentiles.

I Paul, the prisoner of Jesus Christ for you Gentiles ... how that by revelation He made known unto me the secret (Ephesians 3:1, 3).

There are at least twelve and maybe, as Eustace Mills says, some sixteen to eighteen distinct differences between Paul's early ministry before his imprisonment and his later ministry. This is overwhelming proof that Paul had a dual ministry.

Chapter 3

Paul's Unique Latter Ministry (Unique Dispensation - Unique Dynamic - Unique Destiny)

There are three specific areas in which the truth of Paul's latter ministry can be seen.

First of all, we have a unique dispensation. Secondly, we have a unique dynamic. Thirdly, we have a unique destiny.

OUR UNIQUE DISPENSATION

If ye have heard of the dispensation [administration] *of the grace of God, which was given to me towards you* (Ephesians 3:2).

And to enlighten all as to what is the dispensation [administration] *of the secret which has been hidden from the ages in God Who created all things by Jesus Christ* (:9).

Of which I became a servant according to the dispensation of God which is given me towards you to complete [fulfill] *the Word of God* (Colossians 1:25).

To be dispensational in one's interpretation of Scripture is not always acceptable in the realm of theological or church circles. But if we are undispensational, or anti-dispensational, what do we do with Paul's statement in Colossians 1:25?

To be dispensational is to be scriptural, because the word appears in the Scriptures. Twenty times we read these three words: *oikonomia, oikonomos* and *oikonomeo.* Since the word is used so many times, that indicates that we should pay attention to what is being said.

This Dispensation Is Unique
Relative to Its Time

*And you that were sometime alienated and enemies in your mind by wicked works, yet **NOW** hath He reconciled* (Colossians 1:21).

*But **NOW** in Christ Jesus ye who sometimes were far off are made nigh by the blood of Christ* (Ephesians 2:13).

*Even the Secret which hath been hid from ages and from generations but **NOW** is made manifest to His saints* (Colossians 1:26).

I have emphasized the little adverb "*now*" in all three of these verses. This word is usually a translation of the Greek word *nun*, but in these three verses the holy spirit has added a letter, making the word *nuni*. What does that mean? This letter is known as the "iota demonstrative." Thus, *nuni* signifies that at this very moment, not before, not in the future, but *RIGHT **NOW**,* the truth is being revealed.

Nuni puts Paul's statement in a category of

something that is *absolutely* new. God has emphasized it in this one small adverb. Paul is saying, therefore, that *right now* this truth is being revealed: not in the Book of Revelation, not in the Gospels, not at any time before, and not after. The ministry that Paul is talking about here is a revelation given him as a prisoner.

This Dispensation Is Unique
Relative to Its Place

In reading the book of Ephesians, we notice that five times the expression *"in the heavenlies"* is used. We find it in Ephesians 1:3, 20; 2:6; 3:10; 6:12.

There are three spheres of blessing. Some are going to inherit the Earth. Jesus, in His great Sermon on the Mount, said, *"Blessed are the meek for they shall inherit the earth"* (Matthew 5:5).

Others are going to inherit the New Jerusalem. In Hebrews 11:10, 16 we see that *"Abraham looked for a city whose builder and maker was God."* That city of Jerusalem is a satellite that is coming down from heaven to rest upon the Earth in the New Heavens and the New Earth. It is possible that the New Jerusalem will hang in the Heavens like a satellite during the Millennial Kingdom. Then when God comes to renovate the Earth, the city will come down here upon Earth. The point is that there is a special group, different from those who are going to inherit the Earth.

One might ask, how do you know that there are some who are going to inherit the Earth, some the New Jerusalem, and some who will inherit the Heavenlies?

Paul says, with reference to resurrection, *"there are bodies terrestrial and there are bodies celestial"* (I Corinthians 15:40).

Without doubt there are those who are going to inherit the Earth. It could very well be that they will be animated again in the resurrection by a soulish principle, the principle of blood. They are going to be Earth bound.

Then there will be those who are celestial and could very well be animated by the spirit. It seems very clear from the Bible that there are these 3 different spheres of blessing. The

meek shall inherit the Earth. There is a New
Jerusalem. There are the Heavenlies.

OUR UNIQUE DYNAMIC

In Ephesians 2:7 Paul mentions *"the riches
of His grace."* We have a powerful spiritual
force in what we call "grace." God had dealt
in grace in other dispensations. In fact, there
has been grace in every dispensation in a certain sense; but, there has never before been
what is called a *Dispensation of Grace* where
grace is absolutely supreme, the great unique
dynamic. This dynamic is unique because of
the supreme production that comes out of it.

> *That He might **create** in Himself of two,
> one new man so making peace* (Ephe-
> sians 2:15).

> *For we are His workmanship, **created** in
> Christ Jesus unto good works which God
> before prepared that we should walk in
> them* (:10).

The words *"create"* and *"created"* are from the
Greek word *kitzo* which means to make an
original formation. It also includes the idea

of proprietorship of the maker. Our creation is said to be *"before the overthrow[1] of the world."* This predates the present creation.

> *According as He chose us in Him before the overthrow of the world for us to be holy and blameless before Him in love, having predestinated us for sonship through Jesus Christ to Himself according to the good pleasure of His will* (1:4-5)

That is unique for us today. We were in God's mind: chosen, predestinated, before this world was brought into its present existence. If one is a believer, one is an old believer – older than Adam. That is a unique thing in our position today and in our calling. Oh, what riches we have in the grace of God!

Christ's Headship

The unique dynamic of grace brings us this supreme position and production in the new creation: the revelation of Christ's Headship over His Body, and ultimately in Heaven and Earth. This is found only in Ephesians and

---

1.   [*Editor*:] or *"disruption."*

Colossians, making it unique.

> … *Hath put all things under His feet and gave Him to be **Head** over all to the church which is His Body* (Ephesians 1:22-23).

> … *Speaking the truth in love may grow up unto Him in all things which is the **Head,** even Christ* (4:15).

> *Christ is the **Head** of the church, He is the Savior of the Body* (5:23).

> *He is the **Head** of the Body* (Colossians 1:18).

> *Not holding the **Head** from which all the Body by joints and bands having nourishment, ministered and knit together, increaseth with the increase of God* (2:19).

> *Ye are complete in Him Who is the **Head** of all principality and power* (:10).

> *That in the dispensation of the fullness of times He might gather together* [or

"head up"] *in one all things in Christ, both which are in Heaven and which are on Earth, even in Him* (Ephesians 1:10).

This is part of our very unique calling. It is by the grace of God that we have this wonderful position. If everyone would see that, it would eliminate all of the denominations that we have today. There is only one Body for this Head: the ecclesia of which we are members.

Five things are spoken of the Head in Colossians 1:18-19.

He is the Head of the Body, the ecclesia: Who is the Beginning, the First-born from the dead; that in all things He might have the pre-eminence. For it pleased the Father that in Him should all fullness dwell.

- He is the Head – *kephalē*;
- He is the Beginning – *archē*;
- He is the Firstborn – *prōtotokos*;
- He has pre-eminence – *prōteuō*;
- He is the fullness –*plērōma*.

Christ's Fullness

Nothing more completely characterizes the greatness and the glory of Headship than the word *plerōma*, which means fullness, completeness and perfection.

The word occurs five times in Ephesians and Colossians:

> ... *the fullness of Him that filleth all in all* (Ephesians 1:23).

> ... *with all the fullness of God* (3:19).

> ... *the stature of the fullness of Christ* (4:13).

> ... *in Him all fullness dwells* (Colossians 1:19).

> ... *all the fullness of the Deity bodily* (2:9).

The Person of Christ is where all fullness resides. It inhabits, it dwells in Him, the Head.

> *That in the dispensation of the fullness*

of times, He might head up all things in Christ, both which are in heaven and which are on earth, even in Him (Ephesians 1:10).

In this unique dynamic of grace we have not only the production of a new man in Christ Jesus, but we have the Headship of the Lord Jesus Christ Himself.

OUR UNIQUE DESTINY

The unique destiny that we have is connected with Ephesians 3:16, *"the riches of His glory."* As mentioned earlier, there are three spheres of destiny.

Sphere One

First of all, in Matthew 5:5, *"Blessed are the meek, for they shall inherit the earth."* There are those who will have their inheritance upon the Earth. Reading further on in the gospel of Matthew,

When the Son of Man shall have come in His glory ... before Him shall be gathered all nations. He shall set the sheep

on His right hand and the goats on His left. Then shall the King say to them on His right hand, "Come ye blessed of My Father, inherit the Kingdom prepared for you from the overthrow of the world" (25:31-34).

Notice that in these passages nothing is said of Heaven.

Sphere Two

Secondly, we have some other statements. For example in the book of Hebrews,

For he [Abraham] looked for a city which hath foundations whose builder and maker is God (11:10).

Then in the next chapter,

But ye are come to Mount Sion and unto the city of the living God, the heavenly Jerusalem (12:22).

Then in Revelation 21:2,

I John saw the Holy City, new Jerusa-

lem, coming down from God out of Heaven, prepared as a bride adorned for her husband.

Here is a city that is coming down from God out of Heaven and will be inherited by Abraham. We believe that this is the city of the bridal company. Those who overcome by faith, like Abraham, will inherit the New Jerusalem.

Sphere Three

Then we turn to such passages as Philippians 3:14 where Paul says,

I press toward the goal for the prize of the high calling of God in Christ Jesus.

The Greek expression for *"high calling"* is *anō klēsis.* This word is not an adjective, but is an adverb. The same construction is found in John 8:23, *"and He said to them, ye are from beneath, I am from above [anō]."*

There are some of the redeemed who are going to inherit the Earth; some are going to walk the streets of the New Jerusalem; and some who are seated with Christ *far above* all principalities and powers who will reign with Him in the heavenlies.

Some are going to form the Kingdom of priests upon the Earth; some will constitute the Bride of the Lamb; some will be the Body of Christ, with Christ as the Head.

Some are going to constitute the *"sand"* seed of Abraham; others the *"star"* seed; some have their calling from before the overthrow[2] of the world and reign with Christ in the heavenlies.

The apostle Paul tells us that *"the dispensation of God which is given to me for you"* constitutes the glorious fact of *"Christ among you, the hope of glory"* (Colossians 1:25-27).

Solomon declared,

> *The Heavens and the Heaven of Heavens cannot contain Thee* (I Kings 8:27).

In other words, God is seated on top of the Heavens. Thus, Ephesians 4:10 reads,

---

2. [*Editor:*] Or, "disruption."

*He ascended **far above** all heavens.*

Therefore, if we are seated with Christ we are seated on top of the very Heavens. The Body of Christ is going to receive *"the inheritance of the saints in light"* (Colossians 1:12.) That can be translated *"the inheritance of the holiest of all in the light."* This is that unapproachable light spoken of in I Timothy 6:16, that glorious light in which God is clothed as with a garment and in which He lives. What a residence for us as members of His Body!

Some astronomers, after peering into the Heavens with their mighty telescopes, have come to the conclusion that the universe is infinite, and it might well be. We wouldn't be surprised if God is continually creating, that we are going to see the manifestation of His creative power in the time to come and that there will be absolutely no end to the infinitude of God's creation. There is no reason why there cannot emanate from Him in all eternity some new creation. And I think God is going to surprise us with something new and different in our super-heavenly residence.

Moreover, with reference to our destiny there is connected with it a super-heavenly resurrection. In Philippians 3:11 we read, *"If by any means I may attain unto the out-resurrection of the dead."* Paul is pressing toward something here that he did not have before. What he had before was the assurance of a resurrection according to I Thessalonians 4 and I Corinthians 15, and he certainly looked forward to that; but he was pressing toward something different from the resurrection that he had under the New Covenant during the book of Acts. He was pressing toward the special resurrection that is going to take place prior to what is called *"the first resurrection."* Paul was pressing forward to a prior resurrection.

> *If* [since] *ye be risen with Christ seek those things which are above, where Christ sitteth on the right hand of God. Set your affection on things above, not on things on the earth. For ye are dead and your life is hid with Christ in God. When Christ Who is our life shall appear, then shall ye also appear with Him in glory* (Colossians 3:1-4).

Let us lift our thoughts into that which sometimes seems beyond our comprehension. God has said it in His Word; faith can take care of the rest. Accept it and believe it, because God has said it.

Your Part

Now that you have read this book, it's your turn.

If the truths presented here have helped you, don't let these truths die in your hands.

Please write to us and let us know your thoughts concerning its content.

Consider assisting us in getting this book into the hands of those who would be encouraged and strengthened by its message:

- Recommend it to your friends and loved ones.

- Order additional copies to give as gifts.

- Keep extra copies on hand to loan to others.

If you have not read the author's other works, order them today.

We would be honored to have your fellowship in getting this book freely to those who hunger spiritually. We have daily opportunities to send it to pastors, Sunday school teachers, Bible college professors and students, Bible class teachers, and prisoners.

DAILY EMAIL GOODIES™

Do you receive our
Daily Email Goodies™ ?

These are free daily emails that contain short quotes, articles, and studies on Biblical themes.

These are the original writings of Clyde L. Pilkington, Jr, as well as gleanings from other authors.

<u>Here is what our readers are saying</u>:

"Profound! Comforting! Calming! Wonderful!" – NC

"The Daily Email Goodies continue to bless my heart! ... They provide plenty of food for thought." – IL

"I really appreciate the Goodies!" – VA

"Your Daily Email Goodies are making me aware of authors whose names I don't even know." – GA

"I am glad to be getting the Daily Email Goodies – keep 'em coming." – IN

Request to be added to our free
Daily Email Goodies™

If you would like to be added to the mailing list, email us at:
Goodies@StudyShelf.com

Hallman was Professor of Biblical Hermeneutics at Northwestern Bible School (founded by Dr. W.B. Riley) in the 1930's. He pastored the Berean Church of Muskegon, MI (1955-1963) and was on the board of Things to Come Missions. Among others he was associated in ministry with Dr. Harold P. Morgan, Otis Q. Sellers William E. Root, J.C. O'Hair, Charles F. Baker, C.R. Stam, and Russell H. Schaefer.

The Apostle to the Gentiles (Paul, His Life, Labors and Letters)

(#1421) 382 pages, facsimile paperback. *$22.*<u>95</u>

Biblical Hermeneutics

(#1438) "The following notes were first compiled while I was pastor of the First Evangelical Free Church at Minneapolis, Minn. I was invited by Dr. Robert L. Moyer, then Dean of Northwestern Bible School, to teach Biblical Hermeneutics at their evening school. At first, I hesitated because I had not had any full course on the subject. But Dr. Moyer insisted that I should come. He said that he would have his secretary come to his class, take down his complete lecture, and have it typed for me. I could then use them as a basis for my notes and teaching. With this kind offer, I could not very well refuse. So during the years 1932-33, I taught Biblical Hermeneutics at the school founded by Dr. W.B. Riley." 214 pages, facsimile paperback. *$19.*<u>95</u>

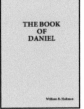

The Book of Daniel

(#1445) 110 pages, facsimile paperback. *$10.⁹⁵*

The Book of Isaiah

(#1452) 66 pages, facsimile paperback.
$8.⁹⁵

The Book of Mark

(#1469) 198 pages, facsimile paperback. *$18.⁹⁵*

Dispensational Distinctions:
Lessons on the Book of Genesis

(#1476) 246 pages, facsimile paperback.
$19.⁹⁵

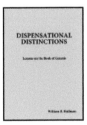

The Epistle to the Hebrews

(#1483) 144 pages, facsimile paperback. $13.⁹⁵

The Epistle to the Romans

(#1490) 66 pages, facsimile paperback. **$8.⁹⁵**

The Great Contrast

(#1513) It is an absolute necessity to "Distinguish between the things that differ" (Philippians 1:10) if we are to escape all of the confusion and the delusion present on every hand. To unite what God has separated is just as gross a violation of His Will and Word as it is to separate what He has united. 36 pages, facsimile paperback. **$3.⁹⁵**

In the Heavenlies: Studies in Ephesians

(#3135) The key to this book of Ephesians is the phrase which occurs five times, namely, *"in the Heavenlies"* (*en tois epouraniois*). It is found in 1:3; 1:20; 2:6; 3:10 and 6:12. It is the dative plural, and in this grammatical construction always means a locality. It is correctly rendered in 1:20, *"in the heavenly places"* or *"in the heavenlies,"* and should so have been translated in all five occurrences. This phrase is found nowhere else in the Scriptures. 70 pages, paperback. *$5.⁹⁵*

The King and the Kingdom in History and Prophecy

(#0646) 42 pages, facsimile paperback. *$4.⁹⁵*

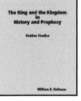

The Short Works of William B. Hallman

(#1506) *Contents:* Complete in Christ; Flowers and Birds of the Bible; From Guilt to Glory through Grace; A Study of the Book of Ruth; In the Heavenlies (Ephesians); Introduction to the Psalms; The Lord's Prayer: It's Historical Place and Dispensational Purpose; A Metaphor of the Mystery: The Body of Christ; Satan's Greatest Surprise; The Unsearchable Riches of Christ in the Dispensation of the Secret; The Uniqueness of Our Calling. 110 pages, facsimile paperback. *$10.⁹⁵*

Compilation Books also containing the writings of William B. Hallman

The Administration of the Secret
(*see listing under Compilations*)

The Creation of Evil, Sin and Satan
(*see listing under Compilations*)

The Lord's Supper
(*see listing under Compilations*)

The Man Christ Jesus
(*see listing under Compilations*)

Enjoy Books?

Visit us at:

www.StudyShelf.com

Over the years we have often been asked to recommend books. The requests come from believers who longed for material with substance. Study Shelf™ is a collection of books which are, in our opinion, the very best in print. Many of these books are "unknown" to the members of the Body of Christ at large, and most are not available at your local "Christian" bookstore.

You Can:

Read

A wealth of articles from past issues of the *Bible Student's Notebook*™

Purchase

Rare and hard to find books, booklets, leaflets, Bibles, etc. in our 24/7 online store.